My Dream

Listen to the Children

John Bougen and James Irving

This book is dedicated to Barbara Edwards, who lovingly inspired all to pursue their dreams.

If one of your dreams could come true, which one would it be?

This was the question we asked the children of the world on our record-breaking, 191-nation quest.

I photographed children at random in every corner of the globe. Their answers were recorded as they spoke, and the children talked with honesty and insight. I have tried to show in the photographs what touched our hearts; we often left with tears in our eyes – mostly tears of hopelessness, occasionally tears of joy.

Above all, we gained an appreciation of how fortunate we were to have encountered children whose dreams and aspirations transcended their everyday lives.

Name

Catalina Carresco
3 years

Location

Corner of Dardignac
and Bombero Nunez,
Santiago, Chile

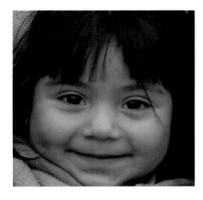

Catalina's dream

"Tener una casa"
(To have a house)

Background

The first photograph of the Quest. Lost and searching
for our hotel in the back streets of Santiago, we asked
two women for directions. Their children were sitting on
a ledge at the base of a wall behind them. We understood
they lived in a shack in the gully at the end of the street.

Matias's dream

"Mi sulno e sir a Worldisney"
(My dream is to go to Disney World)

Name	Location	Background
Matias	Buenos Aires,	Matias helped us out in an internet café … his
10 years	Argentina	computer knowledge far exceeded our own.

"I want to go to the Bandanas' house and stay the night"

Background

Natalia's father Robert, a New Zealander married to an Argentinian, contacted us via the website message board. We met both of them at Cementerio de la Recoleta. The photo was taken just along from Eva Peron's mausoleum. The next day we passed a music store and realised that the Bandanas are an all-girl pop band.

Name	Location
Natalia Mumford	Buenos Aires,
8 years	Argentina

Name

Jose Manuel
Tuainca
13 years

Location

On the Equator,
north of Quito,
Equador

"It's impossible … but I would like to study at university to be a teacher"

Jose's father died when he was very young. He was being cared for at the Institu Museum, where he was learning traditional weaving. No matter how hard we tried, we couldn't get him to smile. When the camera was put away, he opened his mouth revealing that every single one of his teeth was rotten and black with decay. He has never been to school.

Name

Daniel Soltero
13 years

Location

Montevideo,
Uruguay

Daniel's dream

"What is the point of dreaming?"

Background

We despaired of finding a child to photograph on the deserted quiet streets of Montevideo on a Sunday … until we heard the clip clop of the hooves of the horse pulling the Rag and Bone cart. Daniel doesn't go to school, but works full time with his brother on the cart. Neither of them could read or write anything other than their own names.

Name

Gianina Alexandra
Klein Adorni
13 years

Name

Diegdluis Avila
Gomez
13 years

Name

Maria Macarena
Franco Ontano
13 years

Location

Asunción,
Paraguay

Background

All three children were photographed
at a school for the performing arts in
downtown Asunción.

Gianina's dream

"To be a famous violinist"

Maria's dream

"To be a professional
ballet dancer"

Diegdluis's dream

"Please please
please just
take my photo"

"I want to be a singer like Britney Spears"

Name

Ana-Maria Salazar
Boraug,
11 years

Location

Bogotá,
Colombia

Background

Ana-Maria was at the airport with her aunt, who was taking her on a holiday to the States.

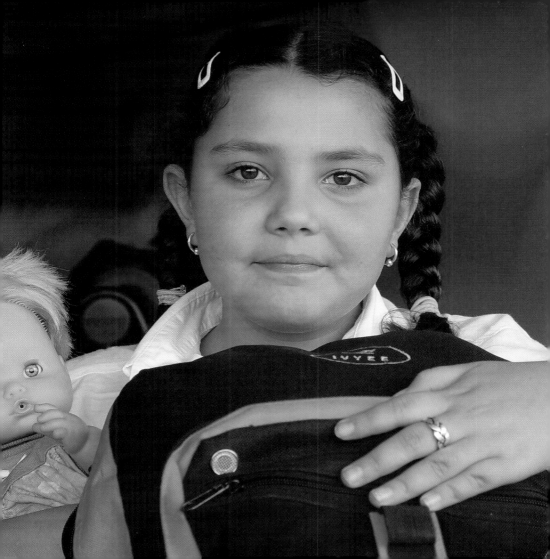

Name

Masiel Saudoral
Saaredra
3 years

Location

Santa Cruz,
Bolivia

Name

Leaudro Taledo Saaredra,
Masiel's twin sister
3 years

Location

Santa Cruz,
Bolivia

Leaudro's dream

"To be a princess"

Masiel's dream

"To travel to England to see my auntie"

"To be a doctor
(gynaecologist) and
help the women of
Grenada"

Name

Rhysia Joseph
13 years

Location

St George's,
Grenada

Background

Rhysia was the only one in a crowd
of students gathered after school in
the central square who was brave
enough to have her photograph taken.

Marlon's dream

"I want my
Daddy back"

Name

Marlon Mapp
3 years

Location

Kingston,
St Vincent

Background

Marlon was absorbed in tracking a
rat as it scuttled from one end of
the drain to the other in front of his
mother's market stall. Following this
excitement, it took quite a while to
get Marlon to stand still. We didn't
like to ask where Daddy was.

Name	Location	Background
Daniella Mitchell 9 years	Port of Spain, Trinidad and Tobago	Daniella was the daughter of our taxi driver, Cleaver Mitchell. The photograph was taken outside the roadside shop opposite her house and her aunt's shop.

"I will like the world
to have peace and
to visit my cousins
in America, and I will
also like to take over
my aunt's business"

Name	Location
Rawle Dalson	Castries,
8 years	St Lucia

Background

Rawle was the grandson and the pride and joy of our taxi driver, who insisted on taking us miles out of our way to find him. The extra fare was worth it for the tour and the experience.

Rawle's dream

"I want to learn well, so that I can get a good job – because I want a car"

Patrice's dream

"I want to go to Disney World"

Name

Patrice Athanaze
11 years

Location

Melville Hall
Airport,
Dominica

Background

A fellow disrupted passenger. Bad weather forced us to overfly Dominica and return the next day, which thrilled Patrice because he was able to spend a night in a hotel and eat in a restaurant.

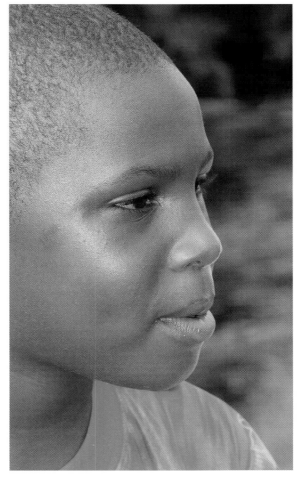

Michael's dream

"To go to Australia
because I like cricket"

Name

Michael
Sookhdeo
12 years

Location

Providence,
Georgetown,
Guyana

Background

We stopped at the Providence Primary School en route
to the city centre. Michael was selected by his teacher
Abiola Liefale because he is an outstanding pupil.

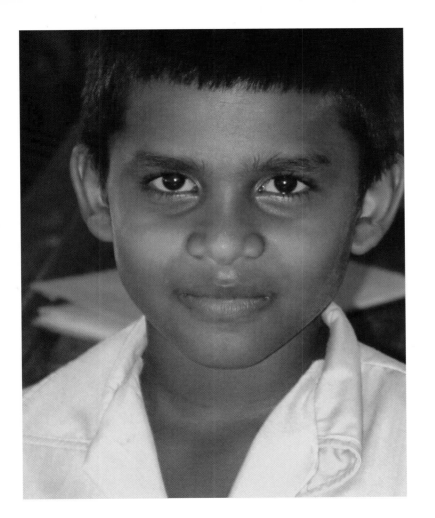

Kareem's dream

"All I dream of
is having a
PlayStation"

Name	Location	Background
Kareem	On board 8B 772	Kareem and his brothers were about as excited as three boys
James	ANU- SKB,	could get on their first ever flight. His mother's view was that
7 years	Antigua	if his dream came true, then he would want for no more.

"To be a worldwide Christian dancer … for my church's touring dance group"

Name

Regine Stanley
11 years

Location

Braseterre,
St Kitts

Background

Regine was in a computer shop gazing wistfully at everything on display while we were there getting our computer fixed.

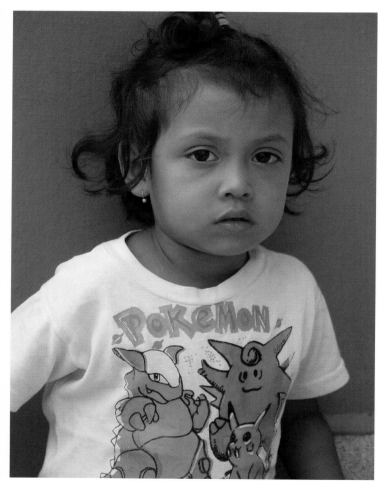

Name

Zolita Eujenia
Shaheta
3 years

Location

Outside the
Gallerias Shopping
Centre,
San Salvador,
El Salvador

Background

Zolita was sitting
quietly to the side of
where her mother was
begging outside the
TACA office at the
Gallerias … as she did
every day.

Mother's dream for her daughter

"That my daughter has the best"

Ella's dream

"I would like to fly away"

"Where to?"

"Anywhere but here"

Name

Ella Janvier
13 years

Location

Petion-Ville,
Haiti

Background

Ella was
photographed
while returning
up a long hill to
her house with
water from the
communal tap.

Shem's dream

"I want a pet lion"

Name

Shem McLennon
6 years

Location

Nassau,
Bahamas

Background

Shem was on
his way to the
library, dragging
his mother
behind him.

Angel Joanna's dream

"To be a model ...
but first I will need a
pretty new dress"

Name

Angel Joanna Elobarus
10 years

Location

Mexico City,
Mexico

Background

A street kid who
with many others
mobbed us in a
park – they all
wanted their
photographs taken.

Camron's dream

"To be a Taekwondo Master, just like my teacher, Master Lee"

Name	Location	Background
Camron Roadman 9 years	Virginia Beach, Virginia USA	Camron had a very troubled upbringing before being adopted when he was 6 years old. Finally, now both he and his home life have settled.

"Not to go to jail"

Name	Location	Background
Elias	Guatemala Airport,	Elias was one of approximately twenty shoeshine
Jose	Guatemala City,	boys at the airport. Stories abound of children
8 years	Guatemala	being "taken away" by the "authorities" in
		Guatemala. Others refer to "the removal".

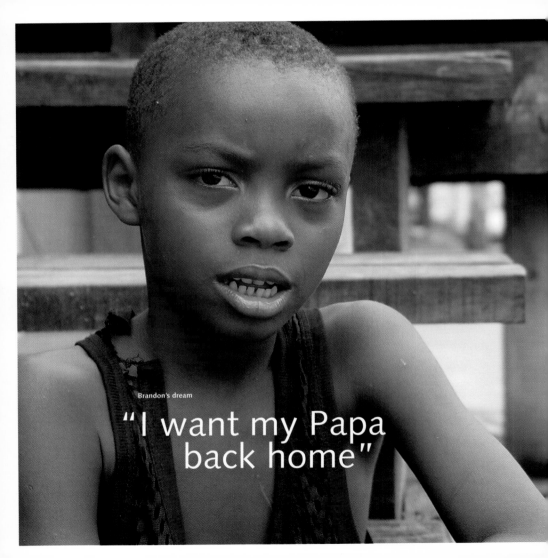

Brandon's dream

"I want my Papa
back home"

Name	Location	Background
Brandon Jeffries 6 years	Belize City, Belize	Brandon's parents have been separated for a year. His mother matter-of-factly stated, "One man can't have two women."

Te Ariki's dream

"To be the ultimate pig hunter"

Name

Te Ariki (Marcus)
Morehu, *(left)*
15 years

Location

Ohau Weir,
Rotorua,
New Zealand

Background

The boys had just
returned that
morning from an
unsuccessful pig
hunt. Their ultimate
catch is a 150kg
"Captain Cooker".

Name

Urukapuarangi (Uru)
Huriwai
6 years

Location

Moerewa Marae,
Moerewa, Rotorua,
New Zealand

Background

Uru was visiting
her grandparents
who live on the
marae.

Uru's dream

"To be a singer and dancer
… because I like singing
and dancing"

"For everybody to be as happy as me"

Name	Location	Background
Karlotta Bhjaltadottir 6 years	Keflavik, Iceland	Karlotta is the sister of the barmaid at the Hotel Keflavik. The photograph was taken in her back garden.

Sophie's dream

"To own a kennel so that I can be with dogs all day long"

Name

Sophie Bjurstedt
11 years

Location

Oslo,
Norway

Background

Sophie's mother Siri works for
Save the Children, Norway.

Mattias's dream

"I want to be the one who finds the cure for HIV/Aids"

Name

Mattias Jehlbo
15 years

Location

Stockholm,
Sweden

Name

Annamaria Wakileh
4½ years

Location

Vienna,
Austria

Background

Annamaria was
photographed at
a shopping centre
with her mother.
Christmas Day
was still very
much on her
mind.

Annamaria's dream

"For every day to be Christmas"

"I want to be happy and healthy forever"

Name	Location	Background
Maiju Roysky 13 years	Fish Market, Helsinki, Finland	Maiju was photographed in the herring market that is set up annually on the waterfront at the start of the herring season.

Chang Ching's dream

"To drive a train"

Name	Location	Background
Chang Ching Hsiang 7 years	Taipei, Taiwan	It was Sunday and Chang's time out with his father in the park.

Genesis's dream

"To fly away"

Name

Genesis Alejandrr
Avila Cabrerr
7 years

Location

Plaza Morazon
(Central Park),
Tegucigalpa,
Honduras

Background

Genesis was
helping her
mother at their
coconut juice
stall. She had
never been
to school.

Sawarsamali's dream

"To see the city ... Colombo"

Name

Sawarsamali
Wijesekam
11 years

Location

Medawala
District,
Sri Lanka

Background

The only modern feature in Sawarsamali's village was the corrugated-iron roofing on some of the houses that had been donated by Japan. The village had no electricity, running water or paved roads.

Resida's dream

"To go to America"

Name

Resida
14 years

Location

Near Buston,
Uzbekistan

Background

During cotton
harvest time, all of
the schoolchildren
in the area go cotton-
picking after school
finishes for the day.
Our presence was a
welcome diversion.

Name

Masquera
14 years

Location

Near border with Buston,
Tajikistan

Background

Just over the border
from Uzbekistan, the
dream was the same.

Masquera's dream

"I want to go to America"

"I want to have very much money so that I can go to Disneyland"

Name	Location	Background
Aysel Akhundova	Baku,	With the ancient city of Baku as a backdrop, Aysel agonised
7 years	Azerbaijan	over her dream. Future dreams of dancing and acting were
		finally dimissed for more immediate fun.

"To be an attorney …
to help my people
get recognised"

Name	Location	Background
Sean Jones (Indian name Eagle Spirit) 10 years	Chesapeake City, Virginia, USA	Sean and his brother are members of the Lumbee Tuscarora Tribe. Along with their parents they had travelled to Chesapeake City Park to participate in the 7th annual American Indian Festival, both an income- and profile-raising event.

"To be happy
like my father"

Name	Location	Background
Hasanov Aykhan Urfan Oglu 11 years	Near Georgian-Armenian border, Georgia	Hasanov was helping his father, the local butcher, slaughter a sheep. They couldn't believe that we found their activities so interesting.

"I want a kitty cat …
a white kitty cat"

Name

Taya Blackburn
3 years

Location

Fairbanks,
Alaska,
USA

Background

Taya was adopted at birth. It was a difficult first few weeks because her birth mother was a cocaine addict. Taya's mother was of Inupiak Athabascan, Japanese and Swedish blood. The story of her heritage was discovered from geneology research, which has to be completed for adoptions. One hundered years ago, in a very bad winter, twins were born to an Athabascan mother and a Japanese father from Yokohama. The smaller child was left outside to die so that the stronger might survive. A couple came along, found the baby and took it to raise in the Alaskan interior. Taya is descended from this lucky child.

"The one thing that I wish for is to share out the world's money ... so nobody has to be poor."

Name	Location	Background
Rebecca West	Lake Pupuke	Rebecca's mother was competing in
12 years	Auckland,	a corporate triathlon, while Rebecca
	New Zealand	was enjoying a more leisurely pursuit.

"To be a judge in the high court"

Name	Location	Background
Rania Nawali	Tunis,	The status of Tunisian women is unique in Africa and the
6 years	Tunisia	Arab world. It was explained to us: "The young women of today do not even think in terms of equality; they have taken it for granted."

"Where's that drink that you promised me?"

Name	Location	Name
Hosia Mviriasgi	Chobe Area,	All of the other children Hosia was playing with were
5 years	Botswana	simply happy to have their photograph taken. Hosia alone pre-negotiated payment for his services.

Jordan's dream

"To play hockey in the NHL … and one day win the Stanley Cup"

Name

Jordan Cyr
13 years

Location

Ottawa,
Canada

Background

Jordan is an
all-Canadian
boy who wants
to go to the top
of his chosen
sport – and no
doubt will.

Pierina's dream

"I want to own my own horse
and all of the equipment, so
that I can win an equestrian
gold medal at the Olympics"

Name

Pierina Hefti
12 years

Location

Flims,
Switzerland

Alissa's dream

"To go back to live in India and have my best friend Harriet there with me"

Name

George Edward Henry
Kirton
15 years

Location

Newcastle,
United Kingdom

Background

George had spent
most of his life
living in Africa and
the Middle East
with his parents. He
had opinions about
many things, in
particular the UN.

George's dream

"To be a UN spokesperson,
so that there is a voice other
than that of the imperialistic
American government"

"To be an engineer so I can build big buildings"

Name	Location	Background
Samy El Ghali Jalal 10 years	Casablanca, Morocco	Samy was the son of the travel agent who issued the tickets for the start of our West Africa travels. He was waiting for his mother to finish work so they could spend the rest of the day together.

"There is so much building to be done in Nouakchott … I want to be an engineer"

Name	Location	Background
Gemal Amara 9 years	Nouakchott, Mauritania	We met Gemal's father, Mohamed, at the Houda Hotel the night before the start of Ramadan. He insisted on giving us a tour of Nouakchott and its hinterlands the next day, culminating in taking tea at his home, and meeting and photographing Gemal. Because of Ramadan, he was unable to join us for tea.

"To go to the States"

Name	Location	Background
Souleymane Diallo	Conakry,	Souleymane was the brother of the driver who drove us around the squalor and deprivation of Conakry. We had tried to photograph children in the streets but were stopped every time … we could only surmise that they were embarrassed about where they were forced to live.
Cosa	Guinea	
Age unknown		

"I wish for good health for everybody"

Name	Location	Background
Alphonsine Palme Prisica 7 years	Ouagadougou, Burkina Faso	Alphonsine is the daughter of the housekeeper at Andy and Lara's house. Andy is a Kiwi who contacted us on our website and, thankfully for us, insisted we stay with them. As we arrived late at night and left at daybreak, we had little time, so were fortunate to meet Alphonsine.

"For my daughter to have a much better life than me"

Name	Location	Background
Nkolouma Anais	Libreville,	Coming out of the tailor's shop in the suburbs of
3 years	Gabon	Libreville, we found Nkolouma and her mother sitting
		beside the road, taking advantage of the cool evening air.

"To choose
my future"

Name	Location	Background
Vickram Lal 12 years	Janpath Lane, New Delhi	Vickram is descended from a long line of mahouts (elephant keepers/drivers). It is expected that he will follow in his father's footsteps. Because of Delhi's traffic congestion, the authorities are trying to remove elephants from the streets. Vickram may yet be forced to choose his own future.

"I want to be a nurse … I want to make people feel better"

Name	Location	Background
Lerato Modise 4 years	Soweto, South Africa	Lerato is named after the hospital where she was born. Her name is a Sotho word meaning "love".

"To get into college without having to have sex with a teacher"

Background

Filomena was worried that to get one of the limited places available for girls in high school, she would have to have sex with a teacher, and possibly contract Aids. There are literally thousands of girls chasing the few female place allocations. At the end of the seventeen-year civil war in Mozambique (1992) there were only six high schools left operating. While 6000 new schools are needed, few have opened, in part because there are only 600 teachers a year being trained. Offset this against the deaths of teachers from Aids, and it is likely to be decades before education is available to all.

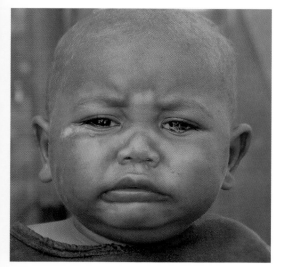

Name

Laline (*above*)
6 years

Name

Fetra (*bottom left*)
2 years

Location

Antananarivo,
Madagascar

Background

The parents of these
children were vegetable
peddlers, their produce
displayed on plastic
cloth on the footpath
of Liberte Boulevard.
While Laline said that
she liked school, she
enjoyed the school
holidays better.

Laline's dream

"To be able to play in the park all of the time"

Parents' dream for their son

"Soon we will be old … we dream that our son will stay strong so he can look after us"

Name

William Njoroge
(*left*)
8 years

Name

Tom Njoroge
(*right*)
5 years

Location

Githurai, Northern
Suburb, Nairobi,
Kenya

"To be an airline pilot so that I can fly across the mountains to Tanzania"

"Earn lots of money so that I can start a school for the local children"

Background

Githurai, a suburb on the northern outskirts of Nairobi, had no sealed roads, sewage, or electricity. Tom and William's grandmother had initiated an assistance group that provided school uniforms and transport for some of the children of the area.

Without this help they could not enter the "free" school system or travel to school. When asked, William could not explain why Tanzania was where he wanted to go, other than he had heard of it, and it wasn't in Kenya.

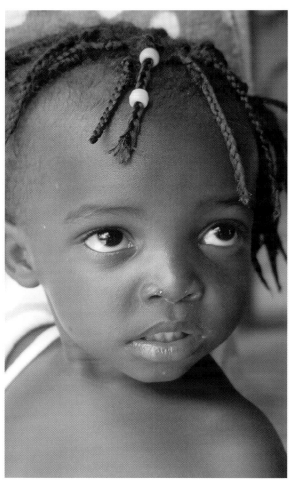

"Life is bad now in Zimbabwe. I pray that for Mandile it is better"

Name	Location	Background
Mandile Neuibe	Victoria Falls,	Mandile's mother was one of the lucky ones as she had
1 year, 5 months	Zimbabwe	a job working for the Victoria Falls National Park. She
		did not have to beg on the streets like so many others.

"To have my own fruit shop, so that I can earn enough to look after my family"

Name	Location	Background
Havyarimana	Bujumbura,	Havyarimana's father died when he was two years old.
Desrire	Burundi	His mother and four brothers continue to live in a village
15 years		100 miles to the north-east. The $3 per month he earns
		from the wholesaler who provides accommodation and
		food for him is the only money the family receives.

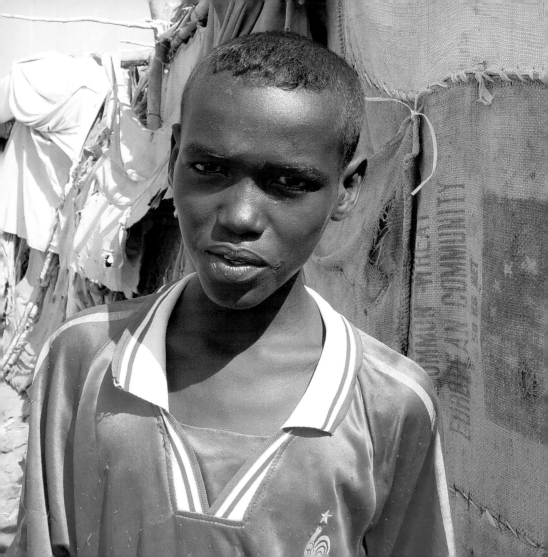

Mohamed's dream

"To somehow go to a better place"

"Where?"

"Just not here"

Name	Location	Background
Mohamed Aydiid Age unknown	Loyada, Djibouti	Mohammed's complete distrust of our motives disappeared when he saw, for the first time in his life, his photograph on the screen of our digital camera.

"To go to heaven after my life is finished"

Name	Location	Background
Gouled Said Dalter 12 years	Lawyo Addo, Somalia	Gouled is the grandson of the village chairman, who was very kind to us. The chairman's enthusiasm for our quest meant we were able to photograph his grandson.

Name

Karim Sadk
10 years

Location

Giza,
Egypt

Background

Karim had been
a beggar at the
Giza pyramids all
of his short life.
He couldn't recall
when he had last
seen his parents.

"I want to be a policeman …
but how is that possible?"

"That he will always be healthy and well"

Name	Location	Background
Athanqsios Boros 3 years	Athens, Greece	Athanqsios was attending the staff children's Christmas party at our Athens Hotel. He was full of sugar and bouncing off the walls.

"For my grandmother to be able to keep thinking of everything for me"

Name	Location	Background
Saedin Alimoski 6 years	Ohrid, on the shores of Lake Ohrid, Macedonia	Both of Saedin's parents "got sick and died" when he was a year old. He lives with his elderly and frail grandmother, who depends on his begging to pay for her medicine. Soon he will be completely on his own.

Saeed's dream

"I want a car ... a black Mercedes"

Name

Saeed
6 years

Location

Wadi Shawaq, south-east of Dubai, United Arab Emirates

Background

The car of Saeed's dream is the most common vehicle on the streets of Dubai.

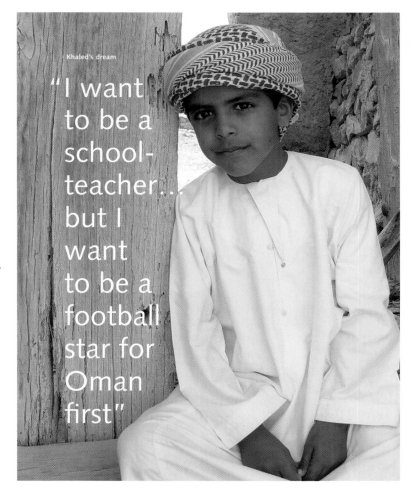

Khaled's dream

"I want to be a school-teacher... but I want to be a football star for Oman first"

Name

Khaled Ali Kholfan
8 years

Location

Ajeep Village,
Shehas, Oman

Background

Visitors are rare at Ajeep. The generosity and kindness of the villagers was only curtailed by the call to prayer, which meant we were alone to explore the nearby old fort.

"To have a house so that I don't have to live under that building over there"

Name	Location	Background
Momani Biswas 13 years	Kolkata, India	"That building over there" was the Airport Authority building, where each night she squatted in the basement with hundreds of others.

Gyem's dream

"For 10 March to come quickly"

Name

Miss Gyem Lham
6 years

Location

Paro,
Bhutan

Background

Gyem was to start
school for the first
time on March 10,
2003. All children
in Bhutan must
attend school.

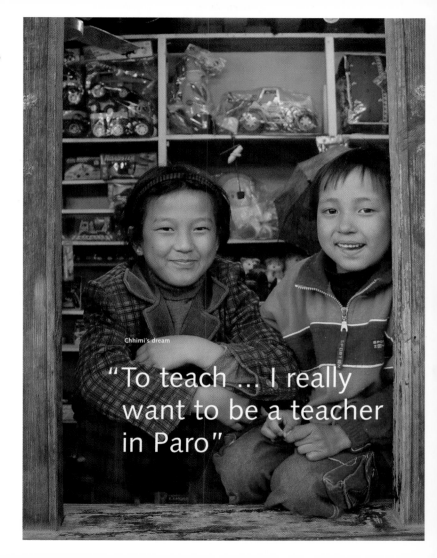

Name

Chhimi Dem (*right*)
8 years

Location

Dechen General
Shops, Shop 55,
Main Street,
Paro,
Bhutan

Chhimi's dream

"To teach ... I really want to be a teacher in Paro"

"Not having
to be here"

Name	Location	Background
Carlos, 7 years	Manila Philippines	Carlos was one of about 100 beggars at the last set of traffic lights before the airport.

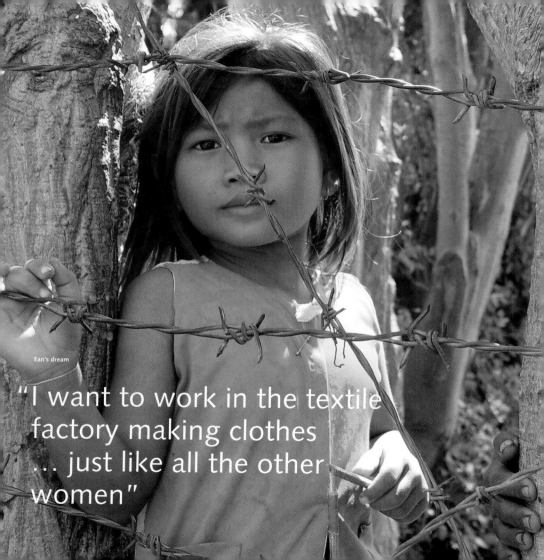

Ean's dream

"I want to work in the textile factory making clothes ... just like all the other women"

Keo's dream

"To be a rice farmer"

Name

Miss Ean
(*left*)
9 years

Name

Keo Pouv
8 years
(*right*)

Location

Chorungek
Genocidal centre,
15 km out of
Phnom Penh,
Cambodia

Background

Part inquisitiveness
and part begging
accounted for the
girls' presence near
the exit from the
chillingly haunting
"Killing Fields"
memorial.

"When I get enough money from begging I will become a shoeshine boy at the airport"

Name	Location	Background
Master Eki Mustakim 12 years	Medan, Indonesia	We gave Eki $US5 which was all he needed to buy the basic shoeshine kit. His dream came true quicker than he had ever hoped. The smile that enveloped his face was priceless.

"The only thing I want to be is a doctor"

Name

Dayangku Nurfatin
Hazmaliyana
9 years

Location

Bander Seri,
Begawan,
Brunei

Background

In Brunei the people appear to benefit to some degree from the nation's oil revenue.

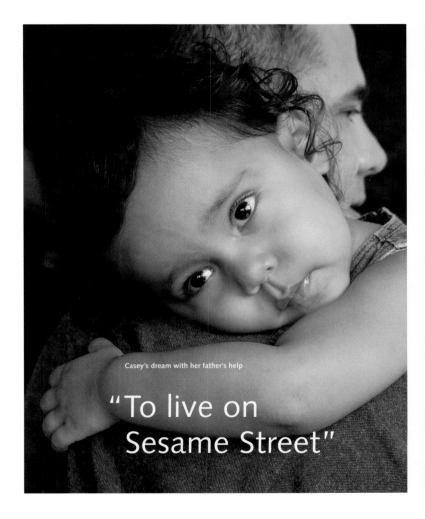

Casey's dream with her father's help

"To live on Sesame Street"

Name

Casey M.
Pangelinan
20 months

Location

Tamuning,
Guam

"That he will have happy, good and healthy parents … and he will be happy with them"

Name	Location	Background
Jokubas Zagorskiese 2½ years	Vilnius, Lithuania	Inga, Jokubas's mother, was taking her son for a walk at about 9 p.m. to try to get him to sleep.

Lee's dream

"To go in a car"

Name	Location	Background
Lee Tan 2 years	Rural village to the north of Beijing, China	As relayed by his mother, Lee, pointing to our car, which is an unusual sight in her village. The sole means of transport for Lee's family was a bicycle. Neither he nor his mother, who was sitting beside him shucking corn, had ever been in a car.

Speedy's dream

"I want nothing...
I have everything that I need"

Name

Speedy Gibkau
10 years

Location

Betio Village,
Tarawa,
Kiribati

Background

We found Speedy in the rubbish
dump hacking apart a battery with a
machete to get the lead out to make
fishing weights. He was oblivious to
the harm that it could cause him by
rubbing his eyes with his acid- and
lead-covered hands.

Tana's dream

"I want to be able to talk to him again"

Name

Tana Otea,
(*third on right*)
9 years

Location

Betio Village,
Tarawa,
Kiribati

Background

Tana's grandfather, her best friend,
had recently died.

"The street kids drink and smoke ... if only they could have a house and family just like mine"

Name	Location	Background
Hapahrob (*top right*) 14 years	Ulaanbaatar, Mongolia	The central square was the location of a recent ice-carving competition. The girls pointed out that most of the children playing in the park were street kids. The temperature was -11°C.

"To travel … I want to see everything"

Name	Location	Background
Valerie Reimers	Majuro,	Valerie's parents owned and managed
13 years	Marshall Islands	the hotel that bore her family's name.

EL NINO

Ayden's dream

"To fly by my bare hands ..." just like Superman"

Name

Ayden Nicolle
8 years

Location

Palm Beach,
Queensland,
Australia

Name

Chloe Nicolle
16 years

Location

Palm Beach,
Queensland,
Australia

Chloe's dream

"To always live by the beach"

"To be a policeman and stop robbers and bad people"

"I want to be a doctor for animals ... and that is possible!"

Name	Name	Location	Background
Ateca Nakawa (*left*) 12 years	Daniela Naruma (*right*) 12 years	Vatukarasa Village, Fiji	Ateca and Daniela were rehearsing with their class for a forthcoming school performance. Our arrival was far more interesting to the children.

Name

Kayla Warsome
7 years

Location

Virginia Beach,
Virginia,
USA

Kayla's dream

"To be a doctor, so I can help
God make people better ...
so they don't get sick
anymore"

Caleb's dream

"Simple ... to be an astronaut"

Name

Caleb Rodriguez
11 years

Location

East Los Angeles,
USA

Background

Caleb's mother Maria attends the Eastside Learning Center where she is learning English. Caleb has taken all of the opportunities that the FLASC programme offers, and that afternoon he had received the prestigious President's Education Award for Outstanding Academic Excellence – hence his smart attire. When he started school he could speak only Spanish.

At FLASC (Family Literacy Advocates of Southern California), families come to school together, attend classes on the same campus and spend one evening a week together in the classroom. Parents learn English, receive their high school diploma, gain other workplace skills and learn new parenting skills.

Many of the parents do not have the language or educational skills to help their children in school. Through adult education and parenting classes, they are better prepared to be their child's first and most important teacher. Their children are offered quality literacy-based education in after-school and Saturday programmes through activities such as homework monitoring, tutoring assistance in all subject areas and through a literacy-based curriculum of fun and interactive recreational activities.

Save the Children are a major sponsor and partner in the FLASC programme.

I will always be indebted to the children of the world who consented to sharing their dreams with a complete stranger.

I owe my eternal gratitude to James Irving, my first cousin and fellow crazy traveller, for without his companionship and planning the All Nations Quest would not have been achieved.

Save the Children New Zealand gave us a truly worthy cause to work with, and we were also assisted by their sister organisations in Norway, UK, Mozambique, Fiji and USA. Our special time in Quelimane, Mozambique, reinforced what we were doing. No matter how much Save the Children benefit from the sale of this book, the money will not be enough. However the carefully planned schemes of this organisation give us hope that one day all children may enjoy at least some of the basics of what we call 'living'.

Bernice Beachman, our guardian angel at Penguin Books, always believed that we would achieve what we said we would do, and Philippa Gerrard in her own inimitable way gave structure to chaos, and Paul Shadbolt at Seven brought all the dreams to life. Geoff Blackwell, Joan Mackenzie and Stuart Hugget gave us heart that we were on the right track and inspired the book's name. Finally, if it had not been for Jill Beasley we would never have been driven to conceive the concept of *My Dream*.

All photographs were shot with a Sony DSC-F707 Digital Still Camera.

For details of the All Nations Quest and the background to what lies within these pages visit

www.mydream.co.nz or *www.allnationsquest.co.nz*

PENGUIN BOOKS

Published by the Penguin Group

Penguin Books (NZ) Ltd, cnr Airborne and Rosedale Roads, Albany, Auckland 1310, New Zealand

Penguin Books Ltd, 80 Strand, London, WC2R 0RL, England

Penguin Group (USA) Inc., 375 Hudson Street, New York, NY 10014, United States

Penguin Books Australia Ltd, 250 Camberwell Road, Camberwell, Victoria 3124, Australia

Penguin Books Canada Ltd, 10 Alcorn Avenue, Toronto, Ontario, Canada M4V 3B2

Penguin Books (South Africa) (Pty) Ltd, 24 Sturdee Avenue, Rosebank, Johannesburg 2196, South Africa

Penguin Books India (P) Ltd, 11, Community Centre, Panchsheel Park, New Delhi 110 017, India

Penguin Books Ltd, Registered Offices: 80 Strand, London, WC2R 0RL, England

First published by Penguin Books (NZ) Ltd, 2003, reprinted 2003
3 5 7 9 10 8 6 4 2

Copyright © John Bougen, 2003

The right of John Bougen to be identified as the author of this work
in terms of section 96 of the Copyright Act 1994 is hereby asserted.

Designed and typeset by Seven

Prepress by microdot

Printed by Condor Production, Hong Kong

ISBN 0 14 301897 3

A catalogue record for this book is available from the National Library of New Zealand.

www.penguin.co.nz

"If to dream is to conceive a destination,
then may the path that leads every child
be signposted and free of lurking dragons.

If only this could be so."

John Bougen, 2003

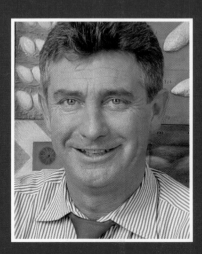